READING POWER

Westward Ho!

Pioneers

Life as a Homesteader

Emily Raabe

The Rosen Publishing Group's
PowerKids Press™
New York

Published in 2003 by The Rosen Publishing Group, Inc.
29 East 21st Street, New York, NY 10010

First Edition

Book Design: Michael DeLisio

Photo Credits: Cover, pp. 7, 8–9, 10–11 © Hulton/Archive/Getty Images; pp. 4–5 © James L. Amos/Corbis; p. 5 (inset) Michael DeLisio; p. 6 Library of Congress, Prints and Photographs Division; p. 9 (inset) © Bettmann/Corbis; pp. 11 (inset), 15 (inset) © Frank Lane Picture Agency/Corbis; pp. 12 (inset), 12–13 © North Wind Picture Archives; pp. 14–15 Denver Public Library Western History Collection, X-14135; pp. 16–17, 18–19 Nebraska State Historical Society; p. 18 (inset) © Hoa Qui/Index Stock Imagery, Inc.; pp. 20–21 © Corbis

Library of Congress Cataloging-in-Publication Data

Raabe, Emily.
Pioneers : life as a homesteader / Emily Raabe.
p. cm. – (Westward ho!)
Summary: Details the lives of pioneers during the westward expansion of the early nineteenth century.
Includes bibliographical references and index.
ISBN 0-8239-6498-1 (lib. bdg.)
1. Pioneers–West (U.S.)–History–19th century–Juvenile literature.
2. Pioneers–West (U.S.)–Social life and customs–19th century–Juvenile literature. 3. Frontier and pioneer life–West (U.S.)–Juvenile literature. 4. West (U.S.)–History–1860-1890–Juvenile literature. 5. West (U.S.)–Social life and customs–19th century–Juvenile literature. [1. Pioneers. 2. Frontier and pioneer life–West (U.S.) 3. West (U.S.)–History–1860-1890. 4. West (U.S.)–Social life and customs.]
I. Title.
F594 .R123 2003
978'.02-dc21

2002002928

Contents

Heading West

Up until the 1830s, most Americans lived east of the Mississippi River. There were thousands of miles of unused land west of the Mississippi River. Over the years, many people traveled west across America to live and work in these unused areas.

Most of the land in the West was prairie. Prairies covered the area from the Mississippi River to the Rocky Mountains, and from Canada to Texas.

The Homestead Act

In 1862, President Abraham Lincoln signed the Homestead Act. The Homestead Act gave 160 acres of free land to almost anyone who was at least twenty-one years old or was the head of a family. The settler had to live on the land and farm it for five years. Thousands of people used the Homestead Act as a way to begin a new life. These people were known as homesteaders.

Many soldiers who fought in the Civil War became homesteaders.

President Abraham Lincoln

Homesteaders came to the prairies from all parts of the country. Some came from the East, where there was no longer enough land for everyone to farm. Homesteaders also came from many other countries, such as Germany, England, and China.

Many people who went to California looking for gold did not find any. Some of them later became homesteaders on the prairies.

Many homesteaders traveled to the prairies in covered wagons.

Living on the Prairie

Life on the prairie was very hard. In the summer, the temperature could be as hot as 100 degrees Fahrenheit (38 degrees Celsius). There were long periods of time when very little rain fell. From June 1859, until November 1860, hardly any rain fell in Kansas and Nebraska. Many farmers' crops died.

In the 1870s, millions of locusts came to the prairies. They ate crops, prairie grass, and the leaves and bark of trees. They even ate leather boots, wooden fence posts, and door frames!

During the summer, long periods of heat could kill a farmer's crops.

Winters on the prairies were very cold. The temperature could reach –40 degrees Fahrenheit (–40 degrees Celsius).

Many homesteaders froze to death in snowstorms. Strong winds blew all year long, night and day.

In Kansas during the winter of 1855–1856, temperatures reached almost –30 degrees Fahrenheit (–34 degrees Celsius). Settlers eating breakfast would find the water in their drinking glasses had frozen.

There were very few trees on the prairies. Since there were not enough trees to build houses, many homesteaders built houses with sod. Sod is dirt covered with grass. Homesteaders cut pieces of sod out of the ground. They used these pieces like bricks to build their houses.

Now You Know

Homesteaders were also known as sodbusters because they broke up sod to build their houses.

[N]EW INVENTIONS

[B]y the 1870s, new inventions made [th]e homesteaders' lives easier. The [m]ost important invention was the [pr]airie windmill. When the windmill [tu]rned, it brought up water from [u]nder the ground. The water was [us]ed for drinking, cleaning, and [fa]rming. Another new invention, [b]arbed wire, helped farmers build [fe]nces cheaply and quickly.

[N]OW YOU KNOW

[Ba]rbed wire was [inv]ented in 1867. By [18]90, barbed wire [wa]s used for fences [on] almost all farms [in t]he western part [of t]he United States.

Sod can be cut into strips and rolled up.

Sod houses leaked when it rained. Bits of dirt and grass also fell into the house from the sod roofs. Sometimes the dirt got into the homesteaders' food. Mice and snakes made tunnels through the sod and into the houses.

Corn was one of the homesteaders' main crops. The homesteaders roasted ears of corn. They also made corn bread, corn mush, and corn pancakes. Homesteaders fed corn to the animals that they raised, such as pigs, cows, and chickens.

Homesteaders also hunted for m
as duck, turkey, buffalo, deer, ro
and squirrel.

Homesteaders did not have wood to burn in their cooking stoves. They used special stoves that could burn dried corncobs, hay, dried cow and buffalo manure, and sunflower stems.

David Haladay invented the prairie windmill in Connecticut in 1854. Before long, homesteaders all over the prairies were using his windmills to pump water for their crops.

Homesteaders turned the prairies of America from empty fields of grass into thousands of acres of useful farmland. The prairies of America became some of the richest farmlands in the world. The homesteaders' hard work changed America forever.

The grass that grew on the prairies was tough and thick. It was hard work to turn prairie land into farmland.

Glossary

acres (**ay**-kuhrz) units of measurement that are used for measuring land; one acre equals 43,560 square feet

Civil War (**sihv**-uhl **wor**) the war fought from 1861 to 1865 between the southern and northern parts of the United States

homestead (**hohm**-stehd) a piece of land in the West that was given to a settler by the U.S. government

invention (ihn-**vehn**-shuhn) something new that someone thinks of or makes

manure (muh-**nur**) animal waste, sometimes put on the ground to make the soil rich for growing crops

prairie (**prair**-ee) a large amount of flat, grassy land with few or no trees

settler (**seht**-luhr) a person who moves to a new country or place

sod (**sahd**) the top part of soil that is covered with grass

temperature (**tehm**-puhr-uh-chuhr) how hot or cold something is

Resources

Books

Life on a Pioneer Homestead
by Sally Senzell Isaacs
Heinemann Library (2001)

Stories of Young Pioneers: In Their Own Words
by Violet T. Kimball
Mountain Press Publishing Company (2000)

Web Sites

Due to the changing nature of Internet links, PowerKids Press has developed an online list of Web sites related to the subjects of this book. This site is updated regularly. Please use this link to access the list:

http://www.powerkidslinks.com/wh/pion/

Index

Word Count: 468

Note to Librarians, Teachers, and Parents

If reading is a challenge, Reading Power is a solution! Reading Power is perfect for readers who want high-interest subject matter at an accessible reading level. These fact-filled, photo-illustrated books are designed for readers who want straightforward vocabulary, engaging topics, and a manageable reading experience. With clear picture/text correspondence, leveled Reading Power books put the reader in charge. Now readers have the power to get the information they want and the skills they need in a user-friendly format.